THE HORN
OF AFRICA

THE HORN OF AFRICA

ETHIOPIA, SUDAN, SOMALIA, AND DJIBOUTI

BY HAROLD AND GERALDINE WOODS

FRANKLIN WATTS

New York | London | Toronto | Sydney | 1981

A FIRST BOOK

Cover design by Jackie Schuman

Photographs courtesy of:
United Nations: pp. 6, 29 (FAO photo by
S. Pierbattista), 32, 49 (FAO), 53;
United Press International: pp. 21, 22, 41;
Wide World Photos, Inc.: p. 27;
Photo Researchers, Inc./Diane Rawson: p. 43.

Maps courtesy of Vantage Art, Inc.

Library of Congress Cataloging in Publication Data

Woods, Harold.
The Horn of Africa.

(A First book)
Bibliography: p.
Includes index.
SUMMARY: Describes the history, geography, and
way of life of four northeast African countries.
1. Africa, Northeast—Juvenile literature.
[1. Africa, Northeast] I. Woods, Geraldine, joint
author. II. Title.
DT367.W66   960   80–22689
ISBN 0–531–04275–8

CONTENTS

THE HORN OF AFRICA

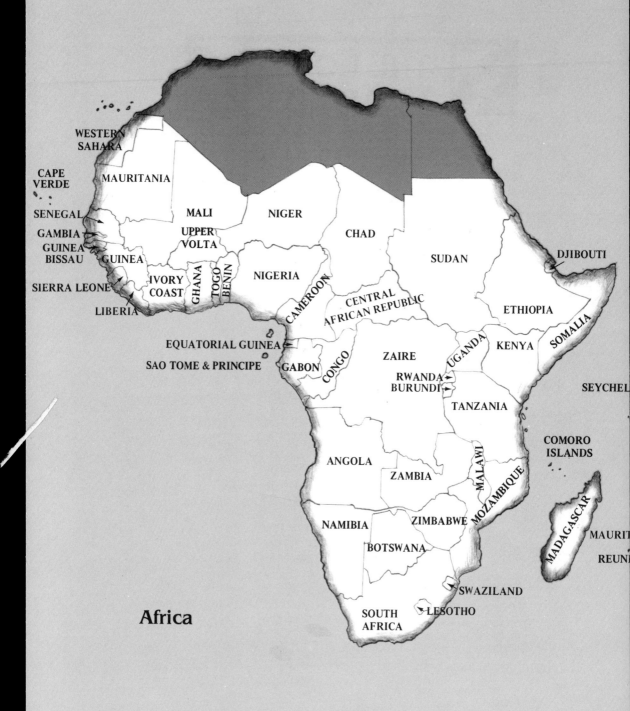

Africa

 **1**

GEOGRAPHY AND CLIMATE

They live in modern apartments, and take buses to their jobs in high-rise office buildings. They live in one-room mud houses, and till the soil as their ancestors did thousands of years ago. They are deep black and light brown, and all the colors in between. Muslim and Christian, they speak over two hundred different languages and wear a variety of clothing that delights the eye. They are all natives of the Horn of Africa, an area that is economically poor but rich in tradition, culture, and the proud spirit of its people. Even the land, which may be snow-capped mountains or parched desert, reflects the variety and beauty of Africa.

Seen from the air, the Horn of Africa looks like a puzzle piece that would fit neatly into place next to the Arabian peninsula, which lies to the north and east of it. Many scientists think that the two land masses were once joined before tremendous forces within the earth tore them apart ages ago. The Horn is now

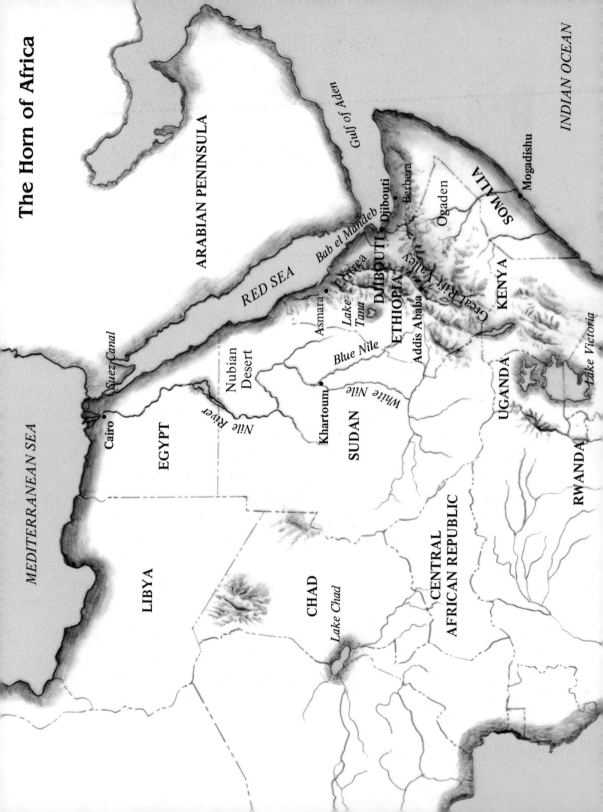

The Horn of Africa

MEDITERRANEAN SEA

ARABIAN PENINSULA

Gulf of Aden

INDIAN OCEAN

Mogadishu

SOMALIA

Berbera

Ogaden

RED SEA

Bab el Mandeb

Djibouti

DJIBOUTI

Eritrea

Asmara

Lake Tana

ETHIOPIA

Addis Ababa

Great Rift Valley

KENYA

Suez Canal

Cairo

Nubian Desert

Blue Nile

White Nile

Khartoum

SUDAN

Nile River

EGYPT

UGANDA

Lake Victoria

RWANDA

LIBYA

CHAD

Lake Chad

CENTRAL AFRICAN REPUBLIC

separated from its Arabian neighbors by the Red Sea and the Gulf of Aden.

Four nations make up the region known as the Horn: Ethiopia, Sudan, Somalia, and Djibouti (pronounced "JUH-boo-tee). With a little effort, the shape of their coastlines can be imagined to be the head and horn of a rhino. It is this shape that gave the area its name.

Two Horn countries, Somalia and Djibouti, form a rough seven along the Gulf of Aden and the Indian Ocean. Tiny Djibouti is the topmost point of the seven, lying next to Ethiopia and across the narrow strait of Bab el Mandeb from the Arabian peninsula. To the west of Somalia is Kenya, which also borders the southern edge of Ethiopia. The remainder of the Ethiopian frontier is shared by Sudan. The largest country in Africa, Sudan is bordered by Egypt and Libya to the north, by Chad and the Central African Republic to the west, and by Uganda and Kenya to the south.

A BURNT LAND

The entire northeast area of Africa is a surprise to those who picture Africa as a dense, humid jungle. In fact, Africa contains almost no jungle at all. There are, however, areas of almost every other type of land—desert, grassland, rain forests, mountains, and scrub land.

The continent of Africa can be compared to an upside-down saucer. Along the coast, where the rim of the saucer would be, is a low coastal plain. Moving inward from the sea the land rises, like the sloping sides of the plate, until the high central plateau is reached.

Around the Horn of Africa the coastal plain is hot, dry scrub land. Ovenlike breezes blow in from the sea, and temperatures can reach as high as 115° F (46° C). Only 2 or 3 inches (5 to 8 cm) of rain fall each year. The Somalis call their northern coastal plain "Guban," which means "burnt land." That is a good description of the coastal plain of this whole area. The soil and climate are so poor that little grows but low trees and bushes.

Inland from the coastal plain the land rises sharply and becomes a high plateau. Part of northern Somalia, sections of Djibouti, and almost all of Ethiopia are highlands. These highlands rise to a height of 15,158 feet (4,620 m) in western Ethiopia. Because of their altitude, the plateaus of northeast Africa have fairly pleasant weather. Temperatures range from 60° F (16° C) to 84° F (29° C), which is quite surprising considering that the northeastern highlands are only a short distance from the equator! Since the cooler temperatures and increased rainfall allow more plants to grow, the highlands contain grasslands, farmland, and even some forests.

Cutting the highlands of Ethiopia into two parts is a valley so large that it is even visible in photographs taken from the moon. It is called the Great Rift Valley, and it extends from the Red Sea straight through to the Republic of South Africa. The Great Rift Valley was formed ages ago when two parts of the earth's surface cracked and slipped. This slippage gave the valley very steep sides. The land within the Ethiopian portion of the Great Rift Valley is mostly grassland, with many lakes.

Other steep-sided river gorges also cut into the Ethiopian highlands. Several mountain ranges, such as the Simen Mountains of the north, divide the flat areas of the plateau. Although beautiful, this landscape is a problem for the Ethiopians. Neighboring villages are often cut off from each other because the journey between them involves climbing a 1,000-foot (305-m) wall of rock!

FOR THE
ADVENTUROUS ONLY

West of Ethiopia lies Sudan, a land whose climate and geography are, with good reason, usually described in travelers' handbooks as being "for the adventurous only." The entire northern section of the country lies within the boundaries of the Sahara Desert. The climate there is brutal, and temperatures often climb past 100° F (40° C). Plant life is scarce because almost no rain falls.

Central Sudan, while not desert, is also hot. More rain falls there, making the region mostly grassland. Southern Sudan, which is called the Sudd, has the most rainfall of all—about 40 inches (103 cm) a year. The land is swampy and the climate hot and humid. Along Sudan's southern border are the Imatong Mountains, an area covered with evergreen forests. Southwestern Sudan is also hilly, with mahogany forests in the valleys.

Except in the desert areas, a great variety of wildlife prospers in the Horn of Africa. The animals most people think of as zoo animals, such as lions, giraffes, and zebras, are plentiful in this region. However, in the Horn of Africa, as in other places, people are expanding their settlements, and the natural habitat of wild animals is shrinking. Today, many African city dwellers see animals only in zoos or on government preserves.

THE NILE

Most people who live in northern Sudan cluster around the Nile River. The Nile actually begins as two rivers. The White Nile, which flows from Lake Victoria on the Tanzanian-Ugandan border, travels the entire length of Sudan. The Blue Nile, which is really brownish-green, has its source in Ethiopia's Lake Tana. It meets the White Nile at Khartoum, the capital city of Sudan, and for a mile or so it is possible to distinguish the separate rivers flowing side by side. The land between the rivers, which is called the Gezira, is extremely fertile.

The Blue Nile River in Ethiopia
spills over the great Blue Nile
Falls and flows into
Lake Tana. The Blue Nile joins the
White Nile at Khartoum in Sudan.

2
ANCIENT AFRICA AND THE EUROPEAN INVASION

Along the Nile in the Horn of Africa, civilization has flourished for thousands of years. Archaeologists have found the remains of a people who lived on the banks of this river over seven thousand years ago. These Stone Age people were hunters, fishermen, and potters. A few thousand years later, in the country now called Sudan, the Nile gave birth to another ancient civilization, known as Nubia or Cush. Historians do not know much about Cush, because no one has ever been able to decipher the Cushite language. However, we do know that the Cushites were rich and powerful, and that they built one of the greatest kingdoms of ancient Africa. Ruins of their temples and pyramids still stand in the Nubian Desert.

Cush had a prosperous trade with Egypt in gold, wood, and slaves. Egypt depended on Cush and eventually took control of it. The Egyptians built temples and pyramids in Nubia, made the people write in hieroglyphics, and instituted Egyptian law. Eventually, Nubia became such a powerful area of Egypt that it was able to conquer its masters. The Pharaoh Piankhi, a Nubian himself, made Nubia the seat of the Egyptian empire.

However, the Nubians ruled Egypt for only a short time. They lost Egypt to the Assyrians, a people from the east who had a well-organized army and iron weapons. The Nubians' weapons were made of softer metals such as copper and bronze and were no match for iron. After losing Egypt, the Cushite Kingdom continued for another thousand years. They developed their own religion, laws, and writing. Learning from the Assyrians, they became skilled iron makers. Their main city, Meroe, became a center for trade from Africa to the Red Sea. Because they used elephants and special decorations, archaeologists have suggested that they traded with countries as far away as India.

AKSUM

Ethiopia was the site of an ancient trading empire called Aksum. As the Nubian kings lost their power, the Aksumites took over their trade routes. By A.D. 300, most of the goods traveling in and out of Africa went through Aksum. Aksum was an impressive city, with large stone buildings and stone needles as tall as 100 feet (31 m). No one is sure why the Aksumites built these mysterious towers.

When Aksum was at the peak of its power, an event occurred which influenced Ethiopian history well into the twentieth century. Their king was converted to Christianity and, as was the custom in those days, most of the king's subjects converted as well. Throughout history, Ethiopians remained true to their Christian religion and glorified it in their art and literature. At one time, twenty-three men of Aksum were employed full time writing copies of religious books. One of these manuscripts was the Bible, which took over two hundred years to be translated into the ancient Ethiopian language of Geez. In the thirteenth century, the Ethiopians built a series of churches as a monument to their faith. Following the king's order, all of the churches were carved out of stone. The largest one, which is still standing today, is called "The Redeemer of the World." It is 110 feet (33.5 m) long, has dozens of windows and two levels, and is made out of a single, solid rock.

FOREIGN INVASIONS
Aksum and Cush became rich and powerful because of trade; trade also shaped the history of the Horn in later times. Because of its location on the Red Sea and the Indian Ocean, the Horn became a gateway for all goods from the Nile valley being sent to the east. When the Suez Canal was opened in 1869, the Horn became important to European trade as well.

As the traders journeyed along the coast, they sometimes stayed and made the African territories their colonies. The history of the Horn of Africa has been determined to a great extent by these foreign invasions.

THE ARABS AND
THE ETHIOPIANS
One foreign invasion took place around A.D. 650 when Muslim traders began to establish trading states in the coastal regions of the Horn. The Arabs mingled with the local people who quickly converted to Islam. However, the coastal lowlands were controlled by the Ethiopians, who were Christians. The Ethiopians allowed the Arabs to live in their territory as long as they paid tribute to the Ethiopian king. The Arabs agreed to this only until they felt strong enough to defy their Christian rulers. Then they waged a series of holy wars to win Ethiopia for Islam. The

Ethiopians were able to fight off the Arab invasion until Ahmed Gran became a sultan of an Arab state. Ahmed Gran was determined to wage a successful campaign against the Christians. He even sold his four wives' jewelry and auctioned off his personal furniture to finance the invasion. His army smashed the Ethiopian forces, and the Ethiopian king was forced into hiding. Towns were looted and churches destroyed. The people of Ethiopia were given two choices: convert to Islam or die. The bloody war continued for sixteen years. Finally, with the help of the Portuguese, the Ethiopians were able to regain their territory and remain Christians.

PRESTER JOHN

The Portuguese had come to Africa in a curious way. As Ethiopia became surrounded by Muslim states, it was cut off from the outside world. Rumors spread throughout Europe about it, but no one knew exactly where, or what, it was. According to one story it was a Jewish state where the Sabbath laws were strictly enforced. It was said that even the rivers had to stop flowing on the Sabbath! Many Europeans believed that a powerful Christian king, Prester John, ruled Ethiopia. He was supposed to have twenty-two kings in his domain. His dining room was said to have magic tables made of emerald and amethyst where people could drink all day and not get drunk!

Catholic Portugal was eager to make an alliance with such a powerful Catholic king. The problem was that no one knew where to find the king. So the Portuguese king sent a number of black women dressed in fine clothes to find Prester John and offer him gifts in the name of Portugal. Not surprisingly, no one ever heard from the women again.

[11]

A Portuguese envoy did reach Ethiopia in 1487. He was treated with respect and given many gifts. However, the Ethiopians had a strange custom. No visitor to their land was ever allowed to return home. So the envoy stayed in Ethiopia and had no way of communicating with Portugal. It took Portugal more than thirty years to find out that they had a representative in the Ethiopian court!

When the second Portuguese mission arrived, they were allowed to return home. Quickly, a great friendship sprang up between the two Catholic powers. Consequently, the Portuguese helped the Ethiopians in their war against the Muslims from the coastal states.

However, the Portuguese soon found out that the Ethiopians were Coptic Christians. Coptic Christians believe in Christ, but are not connected with the Roman Catholic, Orthodox, or Protestant churches. The Portuguese were Roman Catholics. To them, the great Christian kingdom of Prester John was actually a land of heretics. The Portuguese sent Jesuit missionaries to convert the Ethiopians. They changed many of the country's religious practices and forced the Ethiopians to be baptized again. After a few years, the Jesuits were thrown out, and Ethiopia went into another period of isolation. Coptic practices were resumed.

EGYPT AND SUDAN

Sudan was peacefully invaded by Arabs from Egypt in the sixteenth century. At the time the Sudanese were mostly Christian. The Arabs mixed with the local population, gradually replacing Christian customs with Islamic ones. To this day, Sudan remains a Muslim nation.

In 1821, Sudan was again invaded by Egypt, but not peacefully. Mohammed Ali, the ruler of Egypt, wanted to modernize his country. In order to do so he had to build factories and improve crop production. He looked to Sudan to provide the slaves and gold he needed. When he sent his troops south, he found a land of extreme poverty. The people were so poor and undernourished that half of the slaves sent to Egypt died on the way. Mohammed Ali had little trouble taking power.

The Egyptian rule of Sudan was brutal. Villages were burned and the inhabitants slaughtered. Whole areas of Sudan became wastelands. Thousands of refugees, in terror, escaped into neighboring Ethiopia. The conquering Egyptians explored the swampy Sudd and the Upper Nile. The land had large numbers of elephants, and ivory and slaves soon became major Sudanese exports.

In 1884, a Sudanese named Mohammed Ahmed proclaimed himself the Mahdi or Saviour, supposedly sent by God to drive the Egyptians out of the country. Under his leadership, the Sudanese were able to reclaim most of their territory. They began to rebuild their country after years of Egyptian neglect. However, self-rule was short-lived. In 1898, a combined British-Egyptian force easily conquered Sudan with modern weapons. In one battle, eleven thousand Sudanese were killed when they attempted a mass charge against the British, who were armed with machine guns.

OTHER EUROPEAN INVASIONS

Like the British in Sudan, other Europeans had relatively little trouble taking over the coastal regions of the Horn of Africa. The one exception was when the Italians tried to invade Ethiopia. In 1896, twenty thousand Italians climbed the mountains

[13]

of the Ethiopian highlands, planning to attack while most of the Ethiopian army was on a religious pilgrimage. However, their battle plans did not work, partly because no one had ever made a map of Ethiopia! The Italian forces had trouble finding one another. Rallied by their king, Menelik II, the Ethiopians drove the Italians back into the lowlands. The Italian prisoners were forced to build a new church before they were allowed to return home. The defeat of the Italians by an African nation shocked the European world. Ethiopia remained free for most of the period of European colonialism.

The rest of the coastal region fell into European hands peacefully. The Europeans signed treaties of friendship with the local chiefs or sultans. In exchange for their friendship, the Europeans promised protection against Christian Ethiopia. What the local people did not know was that the Europeans were signing treaties among themselves. These treaties were agreements on what part of the Horn of Africa each would get.

By 1925, all of the Horn of Africa, except for Ethiopia, was divided among the Europeans. The British controlled Sudan and Northern Somalia. Southern Somalia and Eritrea were Italian colonies. The French claimed a very small territory north of British Somaliland, the Territory of Afars and Issas, which is now called Djibouti. The Horn of Africa was not to become completely free for more than fifty years.

3
THE MOVEMENT
TO INDEPENDENCE

The nations of the Horn of Africa were not content to remain under European rule forever. Like people anywhere, they wanted to be their own masters. While the colonial period did bring better transportation, medicine, and education, it also brought many problems. Some improvements were made in industry and agriculture, for example, but most of the profits went to the European countries. The native peoples of the Horn were left poorer than ever. The colonial period also sowed the seeds of future wars. Artificial borderlines were drawn by the Europeans, who ignored tribal territories. Some tribes were split up, and others were thrown into the same nation as their enemies. As a direct result of these artificial borders, there is still fighting among the independent nations of the Horn.

SUDAN BECOMES INDEPENDENT

The Muslim Sudanese openly resented being ruled by the Christian British. Sudanese soldiers mutinied, riots broke out in the major cities, and pamphlets were passed out calling for Sudanese nationalism and independence. The British tried to suppress all dissent and stirrings of nationalism in the northern part of the country, and they set up a closed door policy in the South. Travel was restricted between North and South Sudan. All Arabic speakers were forced to leave the South, and Arabic dress and education were forbidden. This closed door policy was an attempt to completely separate the South from the Muslim North, in order to make both easier to control. To an extent, it worked. Today southern Sudanese follow traditional tribal religions and speak their own tribal languages instead of the Arabic favored in the North. This has often led to friction between the two parts of the country.

Gradually, the native Sudanese became more powerful, and the closed door policy was stopped. In 1956, the Sudanese parliament declared Sudan independent. The British went along with the parliament's decision, and Sudan became a free nation. The new country quickly went through a series of coalition governments in which different political parties tried to unite and govern the North and South as one country. However, the Sudanese were unable to agree among themselves about how to solve the problems they faced. The economy was in a poor state, and the South began to rebel against the North.

In 1958, General Abboud staged a bloodless coup. Most Sudanese welcomed the takeover. However, General Abboud was not able to improve the economy, and his bloody southern policy caused tens of thousands of refugees to flee in terror. He resigned in 1964 after a series of general strikes led by students.

The problems facing the Sudanese continued. Finally, in 1969, Colonel Nimieri took over the government. He serves as head of state with support from a cabinet and People's Assembly. Nimieri believes that socialism is part of the answer to Sudan's problems. Under his rule, the government took over the banks, and property was nationalized. Most opposition leaders were either jailed or exiled, and the Communist party was allowed to dominate the country. Recently Nimieri has encouraged foreign investment, and become less strict about forcing socialism on the Sudanese. The South gained more say in its future, and in 1972 a peace treaty was signed with the southern rebels. Though there have been several attempts to overthrow his government, Nimieri remains in power today, making his the longest rule of independent Sudan.

MODERN ETHIOPIA

Ethiopia entered the modern age under the leadership of its emperor, Haile Selassie. Haile Selassie toured Europe, breaking his country's traditional isolation. He instituted a fairer system of taxation, improved education, and made Ethiopia a member of the United Nations. However, democracy did not flourish under his rule. He believed his power came from God, and he made all the major decisions in the country. Under his new constitution, all provincial leaders had to stay in the capital city of Addis Ababa, so Haile Selassie could keep them under control.

In 1934, there was a border incident between Ethiopia and the Italians. The Italians waged a bloody campaign using modern weapons. Haile Selassie was forced to flee, and he spent five years in exile while the Ethiopians fought a guerrilla campaign against the Italians. It was during his exile that he won the sympathy of most of the world. He addressed the League of Nations (a forerunner of the United Nations) and appealed for help for his stricken country. The League, trying to keep European peace at any price, did not heed his call, but his request for justice was supported by other world powers.

In 1941, the British, who were fighting the Italians in World War II, made a general push through northeast Africa. Italian Ethiopia fell, and Haile Selassie assumed the throne. Under his rule, Ethiopia became a leader in African affairs, and an ally of the United States. However, Selassie was not able to resolve border disputes with his neighbors. The Somalis still claimed the Ogaden desert, and the Eritreans did not want to be under the control of Addis Ababa, the capital city of Ethiopia. Both of these territories would later cause much trouble for Ethiopia.

In the 1950s, dissent against Selassie's government began to grow. His subjects became dissatisfied with his absolute monarchy. Educated Ethiopians began to demand a part in their government, a very new idea in Ethiopia, which had been ruled by kings since before the time of Christ. Selassie was able to put down a revolt in 1960, but as he grew older his power lessened. In 1974, a group of army officers called the Dergue (Shadow) officially took control, and Mengistu Mariam emerged as the leader of the Dergue. Since coming to power, Mengistu has attempted to make Ethiopia into a Communist country. He organized the peasants into collective farms, and started health and education programs. However, all opposition to his Communist program is brutally suppressed; tens of thousands of people have been arrested and thousands more executed.

SOMALIA AND DJIBOUTI

During their rule of Somalia, the Europeans met little resistance from the native peoples of the area. However, one remarkable

Somali, Mohammed Abdullah, tried to unite the Somalis and expel the British in a twenty-year guerrilla campaign. Although he failed, he is honored today as a national hero of Somalia.

The Somalis had a particularly difficult time winning their independence because they were a divided people. The European-drawn boundary lines had left some of the Somali tribe in British Somaliland, some in Italian Somaliland, and the rest in Ethiopia, Kenya, and present-day Djibouti. In 1960, Italian and British Somaliland received their independence and became Somalia, under the leadership of a political party called the Somali Youth League. The capital of the new country was established at Mogadishu. As in other newly independent countries, attempts at forming a coalition government failed. In 1969, General Siad Barre staged a coup, and established a new government called the Supreme Revolutionary Council. Somalia is now a socialist state, where all political parties are illegal and most businesses are controlled by the government.

On June 27, 1977, the last European colony in the Horn received its independence. The French Territory of Afars and Issas became the Republic of Djibouti, with Hassan Gouled Aptidon as the first president. The Republic of Djibouti is now ruled by the President, a Council of Ministers, and a Chamber of Deputies elected by the people.

ERITREA AND THE OGADEN

The question of which country owns what land is still unresolved in the Horn of Africa. In January 1975, a rebellion broke out in the Ethiopian province of Eritrea. For centuries, the lowlands of Eritrea and their Christian neighbors were enemies. King Menelik II allowed the Italians to keep Eritrea after he defeated them in 1896. The Italians lost the province during World War II, and the Ethiopians annexed it in 1962. Mostly Muslim, the Eritreans claim that their Christian rulers give them few rights. They wish to be an independent state. After five years of fighting, the Eritrean independence movement has not been crushed. However, the Ethiopian ruler, Mengistu, has vowed to wipe out the rebels. The fighting is still going on.

Another war is being fought in the Ogaden desert of Ethiopia. Siad Barre's Somali government wishes to unite all Somalis, no matter where they live. Since most of the inhabitants of the Ogaden are members of the Somali tribe, Somalia wishes to rule there. Somalia sent aid to the rebels in the Ogaden, and in 1977 launched an official invasion. Siad Barre's troops were successful until the Soviet Union and Cuba decided to send soldiers and supplies to aid the Ethiopians. The Somalis, vowing to return, retreated from the Ogaden desert in 1978, but guerrilla warfare in the Ogaden continues.

The fighting in Eritrea and the Ogaden has created a refugee problem of tremendous proportions in the Horn of Africa. In the past few years, over 20,000 people have entered Djibouti. Another 45,000 have settled in Sudan, and over a million have

With a child strapped to her back, a Somalian woman welcomes members of the Western Somali Liberation Front to her village, which had previously been occupied by Ethiopian troops.

*During a major famine in the early seventies, an
estimated 200,000 Ethiopian people died of starvation.
Hundreds of people continue to die every day in
Ethiopia's famine stricken provinces of Wollo and Tigre.*

fled to Somalia. In Ethiopia, driven by war and crop failure due to drought, over a million people have gone to live in refugee camps. Most of these displaced persons are on the verge of starvation, with no homes, few possessions, and no means of earning a living. The Horn countries, with the help of the United Nations and others, are trying to provide food and housing for the refugees. However, the situation remains serious.

ETHIOPIA

Ethiopia today is an uneasy blend of tribes, languages, and customs. Although the Amharas, the traditional ruling class, have lost much of their power, Amharic, their language, is still one of the official languages of Ethiopia. The other is English. All of the tribes, no matter what their native language, must speak either Amharic or English to deal with government officials.

The Tigre and Tigrinya are also important groups. The Tigre come from northern Eritrea, and the Tigrinya from Tigre province. They have their own languages, which are related to Amharic. Most members of these three tribes are farmers. Physically, they tend to be tall and slender with dark skin. Their facial features are shaped like those of Europeans.

A large ethnic group in Ethiopia is the Galla tribe. Gallas live mostly in southern Ethiopia, and make their living as herders. A large number of Gallas are nomads who wander from place to place looking for grazing land for their animals.

There are several other smaller tribes in Ethiopia. Like the Eritreans, many feel they are not treated properly by the central government and are fighting for more power. At one point, in late 1978, there was fighting in eleven of the country's fourteen provinces.

RELIGION

Ethiopia has a rich religious tradition that is different from anywhere else in the world. The Amharic, Tigre, and Tigrinya tribes are mostly Christian. Their church is the Ethiopian Orthodox Church, or Coptic Church, and is related to the Christian churches in Egypt, Syria, and Armenia.

The Coptic Church has many unique customs. For example, shoes must be removed before entering a church. Some churches do not permit women to enter. Christmas, which is celebrated on January 7, is an unimportant holiday. However, "Timkat," the Epiphany, needs two whole days for all the parties and ceremonies that are held. Coptic services are very dramatic. In one part of Ethiopia, during Lent the deacon rides to church on a donkey. Along the way to the service he is met by people singing and praying in the street.

Many members of the Galla tribe follow the ancient beliefs of animism. Animists believe that spirits dwell in natural things like plants, animals, and rocks. Various ceremonies must be performed to please these spirits, or they will bring harm to the people. In some Ethiopian villages, for example, food is left outside for the King of the Hyenas, who is feared because of his magical powers. He will not harm the village only if he is given enough food.

Another group are the Falashas, or black Jews of Ethiopia. The Falashas have always claimed to be descended from the Tribe of Dan, a lost tribe of Israel that vanished twenty-seven

[25]

hundred years ago. They follow the Old Testament, but know nothing of the Talmud, or Jewish law. In 1975, the government of Israel recognized the Falashas as true Jews and urged them to move to Israel. Few did so, although they have suffered greatly in Ethiopia. Because they work with metal, which Ethiopians consider a tool of Satan, the Falashas have often been feared as devils.

About 40 percent of the people of Ethiopia are Muslims, who also have interesting customs. Those who belong to the Danakil tribe, for example, believe that a man must marry his aunt's daughter. If another man marries her, the nephew must kill him. If his aunt has no daughter, he may marry whomever he likes. The newlyweds go on a honeymoon for forty days accompanied by thorns, palm leaves, and camel dung. The thorns symbolize food, the palm shelter, and the dung the money a man has when he owns a large herd of camels.

WAY OF LIFE

The small minority of Ethiopians who live in cities are likely to find that their lives have much in common with city dwellers the world over. In the capital city, Addis Ababa, for example, blocks of modern houses, apartments, and high-rise office buildings give the city a cosmopolitan air. Small blue and white taxis and public buses clog the streets, carrying residents to their jobs or to such urban delights as the theater, restaurants, or nightclubs. Addis Ababans also enjoy several museums, such as the Museum of Natural History, and a modern zoo. Yet Ethiopian cities are still a blend of old and new. Even amid the glass and steel structures of the capital many one- or two-room mud houses are still found. In Asmara, one of the largest towns in the coun-

*A modern section of Asmara, one
of the largest towns in Ethiopia.*

*A tukul hut is the traditional housing
for peasants in Ethiopia. Tukuls are made
of stone and clay with thatched straw roofs.*

try, horse carts and bicycles compete with motor vehicles for space on the city streets.

The majority of Ethiopians, however, are far removed from the bustle of city life. In the countryside, life proceeds at a slower pace, and the people follow centuries-old customs. Peasants from many areas of Ethiopia still live in traditional houses called "tukuls." Tukuls are round and made of stone and clay, with thatched straw roofs. Inside, in a small hole, a cooking fire is built. Beds are made of animal hides stretched on frames or laid on earthen piles. A table, some stools, and cooking utensils complete the Ethiopian peasant's home furnishings.

Peasants wear shamas, the traditional clothing of Ethiopia. Shamas, worn by both men and women, are thin, white, cotton outfits that look like Roman togas and can be draped in a number of ways. Even sophisticated city dwellers who have adopted Western fashions often wear shamas on top of their modern clothes because they are so beautiful.

Ethiopia's distinctive style is also seen in the favorite national foods. It may be the only place in the world where dinner guests eat not only the food but also the tablecloth! A typical meal might include a fiery hot stew called wat, accompanied by soft cheese wrapped in banana leaves. The dinner is eaten at a round straw table that is covered with a flat, spongy bread called injera. No dishes are used. Instead, the food is placed in little piles on top of the bread. Each person breaks off a small piece of bread, scoops up some stew, and eats!

THE ARTS

Poetry, music, and dance are the favorite forms of expression of the Ethiopian people. Classical poetry is written mainly in Geez, the language of the ancient peoples of Aksum. Although it is no longer spoken, Geez is still used for services in the Coptic Church.

Music is very important to the Ethiopian people. Even in the smallest of villages, people relax and listen to traditional Ethiopian songs. Every celebration is accompanied by music and dancing. The dances vary from tribe to tribe, and some are performed by entire villages. Some dances are important in religious ceremonies. For example, when an Eritrean bride arrives at her wedding, she begins to dance. She must continue to dance until her strength is gone and she collapses. It is only then that she is allowed to see her groom for the first time.

Ethiopian musical instruments are also interesting. The masenko, a stringed instrument, is supposedly a forerunner of the violin. Sistras, rattles similar to ones used in ancient Egypt, and drums are both frequently played too.

There are many exciting Ethiopian games. Yeferas Gooks, one such game played on important occasions only, has teams of horsemen facing each other across a field. The horsemen charge one another, wielding lances like medieval knights.

ECONOMY AND DEVELOPMENT

Although three thousand years old, Ethiopia faces many of the same problems as the newest nations of Africa. Its people are very poor, with an average yearly income of less than one hundred dollars. Poor health care and a lack of education and industry also concern Ethiopians today. The wars in Eritrea and the Ogaden, and unrest in other provinces, have taken time, energy, and money away from these problems.

There is very little industry in Ethiopia. The backbone

of the economy is agriculture. Cereals, such as wheat, a grain called teff, and barley, are grown, as well as sugar cane, spices, tobacco, and cotton. The most important crop is coffee. The Ethiopian city of Kaffa claims to be the birthplace of coffee. Today coffee makes up half of the country's exports.

About 90 percent of the people of Ethiopia make their living by farming, but only 15 percent of the fertile land is now being cultivated. Although the government hopes to develop more farm land, and to modernize farming methods, for the most part, Ethiopians now rely on the backbreaking, primitive ways of farming that their ancestors used two thousand years ago. Insect control is a large problem and farmers often lose much of their crop to pests like locusts. Drought can also cause widespread crop failure and today Ethiopia faces starvation due to this problem. Hundreds of thousands of people are affected— far more than the international relief effort can adequately deal with.

Another major Ethiopian industry is livestock. Sheep and goats are raised, as well as cattle, horses, mules, and camels. Animal hides are an important export.

Ethiopia has not yet taken advantage of its natural resources. At present, only gold is mined in any quantity, but geologists have found deposits of oil and natural gas near the Red Sea coast. However, the civil war in Eritrea has so far prevented their development.

HEALTH AND EDUCATION

Besides making economic improvements, the Ethiopian government hopes to develop the country's health system. Although there are good hospitals in the major cities, medical care is often

*Coffee beans, Ethiopia's most important crop, are
being sorted by workers at a cleaning plant
in Addis Ababa, Ethiopia's capital city.*

lacking in rural areas. Many people are also unaware of how to prevent and fight disease. It is a custom, for example, to eat raw meat in Ethiopia. This results in tapeworm and other parasites. Few homes have toilets, and poor sanitary conditions can spread disease. When a serious illness does strike, villagers do not have modern methods to treat it. The traditional remedy for any illness was to lock the patient in a dark room with a roaring fire. Other cures involve placing magic symbols on a plate.

Fortunately, the situation is improving. Doctors and nurses, often traveling by mule, try to visit all remote areas. Medical workers also instruct villagers about child care and good hygiene. Since a large portion of its budget goes to build clinics and train doctors and nurses, Ethiopian health care will hopefully get better and better.

Education is also improving. Until the 1930s, most school children learned little more than how to read the Gospels and Psalms in the official church language of Geez. There were few primary schools and almost no secondary schools. Now, about eighty thousand Ethiopian children are in primary schools. They study in the official language of Amharic until the third grade, and then in English. However, education in Ethiopia still has a long way to go. Only a few thousand children continue to study at the high school level. There are, however, many technical and vocational schools for adults, and universities at Addis Ababa and Asmara.

5
SUDAN

The ancient land of Cush has become the largest nation in Africa today. As in most African countries, there is no one single tribe of people. Instead, Sudan's eighteen million people are divided into almost six hundred separate social groups, each with its own customs, each contributing in its own way to the development of the nation.

Most of the tribes in northern and central Sudan speak Arabic, the official language of the country. They are descended from natives and Arab traders who moved to Sudan long ago. Although all the Sudanese are dark-skinned, the northern tribes tend to be lighter in color because of their intermarriage with Arabs. The majority of the people in northern Sudan live near the banks of the Nile River, which runs the whole length of the country. They make their living by farming. A few groups, like the Beja of the Red Sea area, are herders and live a nomadic life, traveling constantly looking for food for their camels and sheep.

Among the southern tribes, more than one hundred different languages are spoken. Many southerners also speak Arabic as a second language; some people prefer English as their second language. Many can speak only in their native tongue. The tribes of the southern region, such as the Dinka, Nuer, and Shilluk, do not have Arabian ancestors, but are descended from African blacks. Some are farmers, others are herders who concentrate on cattle rather than sheep or camels.

RELIGIONS, CUSTOMS, AND DAILY LIFE

The Arabic-speaking peoples of northern and central Sudan are almost all members of the Muslim faith. Most of the southern tribes are animists. Although the Muslims hold the same religious beliefs, each tribe practices animism in its own way. The Nuer, for example, believe in Spirits of the Above and Spirits of the Earth. They never eat birds, because they believe birds contain evil spirits. The Nuer often make sacrifices to ward off the "evil eye," which they believe causes death and sickness.

The Nuer also have special ceremonies to mark the day that a boy becomes a man at the age of seven or eight. At that time, several lines are cut into his forehead with a sharp knife. The young man proudly wears the scars from these cuts for the rest of his life. Other tribes also give scars as a sign of maturity. The Dinkas mark both boys and girls. The Nuba, who wear very little clothing, decorate their whole bodies with patterns of scars.

In northern Sudan, meals are important social occasions. Guests are offered fruit juice when they enter a house, and water is poured over their hands into a basin to wash off the dust of the road. Dinner, served in small bowls on large trays, is likely to be spicy hot soups and stews made from onions, tomatoes, other vegetables, and perhaps eggs and meat. Spoons are supplied for soup, but otherwise bread is used to scoop up the food. Coffee is an important part of the meal. The coffee beans are fried in a special pot over charcoal and then ground with cloves and other spices. After it is brewed, the coffee is strained through a fresh grass sieve and served in tiny cups. In southern Sudan, some people prefer tea. The Sudanese eat many vegetables and fruits and brew beer from a grain called eleusine.

An increasing number of Sudanese wear Western clothing, although many continue to use a traditional costume, which varies from region to region. For northern Sudanese men, it is a loose, white cotton robe and turban. Women may wear colored robes, and usually draw a veil over their faces in public.

Housing in Sudan reflects the variety of lifestyles of its people. Many Sudanese who live in cities such as Khartoum and Omdurman, for example, have modern houses. Some of these are impressive brick buildings with efficient sewage systems, air conditioning, and other comforts. Others are simple bungalows located on pleasant, tree-lined streets. The people who live in these homes tend to have Western furnishings, and to wear Western clothing. They may be students in the University of Khartoum, or work in up-to-date offices, manufacturing plants, or government ministries. Yet not all Sudanese city dwellers follow such a modern lifestyle. Even in the capital city of Khartoum, rows of mud houses are still found. These humble buildings do not have modern plumbing. Instead, wastes are carried away each day by camel-drawn carts. In such areas, donkeys are frequently seen carrying goods to large, open-air markets.

In rural areas, the majority of people live in traditional houses. The nomads of the northern desert, who are always on the move, live in tents. The floor of the tent is covered with rugs and sheepskins, protecting the people within from the hot desert sand. Meals are cooked outside over an open fire. The Dinka tribe of the south build circular huts on stilts. The raised house keeps animals out.

It is in the Nuba Mountains that the most interesting and complex dwellings are found. The tribes who live there build compounds for each family. These compounds are made of five stone towers, placed in a circle and joined by a stone wall. One stone tower is for storage, one for animals, one for sleeping, one for grain, and one for water. Cooking is done in the center of the circle, where there is also an outdoor shower. Men in this tribe are permitted to have more than one wife—but only if they build a circle of towers for each!

ARTS AND PASTIMES

Of all the arts, the music and literature of the Sudanese are especially beautiful. Sudanese writing, for example, is very popular throughout the Arab world. Their poetry is especially moving and is often set to music. Singers will praise their homeland, or long for a girl whose eyes are "as large and as black as a cup of Sudanese coffee." There are also songs about famous heroes, relating tales of their deeds. In one poem, written during the colonial period, the singer relates how a peasant refused to pay taxes to his white masters. The desire of the Sudanese to be free and independent is the message of this poem.

The music of these songs is played on mandolins, flutes, and bongos or other drums. From time to time during a performance, listeners may get up and dance or snap their fingers in rhythm with the music.

Dancing is popular on any occasion in Sudan. In every tribe, an important event, like a birth, marriage, or death, is marked with singing and dancing. Some of the dances are very exotic to watch. The people of the Nuer tribe, for example, have a special dance during which the boys paint their faces white and carry spears. Girls, wearing beads and skirts made of leather strips, dance in a line opposite the boys. The boys point their spears at the girls, but do not throw them!

The Sudanese also amuse themselves watching television. Television is relatively new in Sudan, and those people who own sets are likely to find themselves with many visitors during the hours of programming. In some places, the television is set up outdoors and as many as a hundred people gather to watch. Radios are more common and provide news and entertainment to people in rural areas.

Some of the most popular broadcasts on radio and TV are sporting events. The Sudanese enjoy football, which is the game we call soccer, as well as basketball and boxing. While their elders watch these sports on TV, children play their own games, such as *Shedat*. In this game, one player is the bride. The bride's team tries to get her to home base, while the opposing team attempts to steal her away. The game is made more interesting by the rule that no one may run or walk. Only hopping is allowed!

A DEVELOPING LAND

Sudan is primarily an agricultural country, and it is in this area that progress has been most notable. Probably the greatest success story is that of the Gezira. The largest farm in the world, the Gezira is located on 2 million acres (808,000 hectares) of land between the White and the Blue Niles.

In the 1920s, British engineers noticed that the Gezira is perfectly set up for irrigation. The area is very flat and tilts gently away from the shores of the Blue Nile. The engineers knew that if the water level of the river was raised a little, it would overflow its banks onto the flat Gezira plain, irrigating any crops planted there. The Sennar Dam was then constructed. The newly irrigated Gezira land was rented to tenant farmers, and cotton was soon planted. Cotton has now become Sudan's major crop, accounting for about half of the country's exports.

Progress, however, brings its own problems, too. Since Sudan does not have many exports other than cotton, the Sudanese economy suffers if the price of cotton on the world market falls. Because of Sudan's one crop economy, the government has been encouraging farmers to plant a greater variety of crops. Groundnuts and wheat are now exported, and vegetables and grains are grown for use within the country.

The Jonglei Canal, a project even more ambitious than the Gezira, is now being built in southern Sudan. When finished, the Jonglei will be longer than the Panama and Suez Canals combined. The Jonglei will drain the swamps of southern Sudan and carry the water to northern Sudan, making 400,000 acres (162,000 hectares) of desert fertile and green. Sudan may be able to grow enough food to deserve the title "Breadbasket of the Arab World."

Sudan also harvests gum arabic from acacia trees. Gum arabic is a sticky substance that oozes from the tree and hardens into chunks the size of walnuts. It is used in the manufacture of ink, candy, perfume, and other products. Sudan supplies over 90 percent of the world's gum arabic.

Other major occupations in Sudan include herding, farming, and fishing. Practically all of the Sudanese who are not farmers make their living by raising cattle, camels, or sheep. Fish are abundant in Sudan's rivers and in the Red Sea but at present, very little fish is exported; most is consumed within Sudan. There are, as yet, few other industries in the country, and manufactured goods must be imported. The majority of people in Sudan, as in the rest of the Horn countries, are relatively poor. Their average yearly income is less than three hundred dollars.

HEALTH AND EDUCATION

A major concern in Sudan is health. Because of the heat and humidity in southern Sudan, disease-carrying insects thrive. There are over sixty types of mosquitoes in the Sudd, and many other pests as well. In northern Sudan, the desert climate also encourages certain illnesses like meningitis and sunstroke. Complicating the problem is the fact that Sudan's many nomads often spread disease over a wide area since they travel so much. Moreover, the water supply is impure in some parts of the country. Doctors and nurses are needed and hospitals are

A donkey carries this Sudanese midwife to a nearby village where she will assist in a child's birth.

This young Beja girl studies English as well as Arabic, the official language of Sudan. Like many Beja women, she wears her hair in fine braids.

few and far between. When Sudan became independent in 1956, there were only forty-nine hospitals in the entire country.

The Sudanese government is attacking the problem of poor health in a variety of ways. Pesticides are being used to wipe out mosquitoes and other insects that carry germs. More health workers are being trained, especially medical assistants, who take charge when there is no doctor available. Clinics and hospitals are being built, as well as mother-child health centers. In these health centers midwives deliver babies and teach mothers how to care for them. In this way Sudan is hoping to build a healthier future.

Education is also improving in Sudan. Before the nineteenth century, the only schools in existence were Khalwas, or Muslim religious schools. Only boys could attend, and the purpose of the education was to learn to recite the Koran (the Muslim sacred book) by heart. Reading and writing were taught only as an aid in remembering the Koran. In the early nineteenth century, some arithmetic, grammar, and history were added to the course. Under British rule, education was again expanded, and nonreligious schools were set up. In 1940, girls were allowed in school for the first time.

Today, Sudan's educational system is expanding rapidly. New schools are being built constantly. However, there are still not enough schools for all children. Teachers are now being assigned to the nomadic tribes. They follow the tribe from place to place, and when camp is made, they set up a tent and begin lessons.

6
SOMALIA

Unlike many African countries, the Somalis are a united people. Almost all of the three and a half million people who live in Somalia belong to the Somali ethnic group, speak the Somali language, and believe in the Muslim religion.

There are two main groups in the country: the Saab and the Somaal. These groups received their names from two brothers, who are believed to have belonged to the tribe of the prophet Mohammed. According to the legend, all present-day Somalis are descended from one of these brothers. The Saab are mostly farmers, and the Somaal raise livestock. Both Saab and Somaal, however, consider themselves part of the larger Somali tribe.

Somalis have traditionally divided their tribe into large family groups called clans. The average clan contains about one hundred thousand people, all related to each other through their fathers. In the past, the clans have taken the responsibility for the widowed, sick, and orphaned of their group. In time of drought, members of the clan would help those of their group who were most in need. Land was also divided according to clan.

For settled farmers, that meant that all the fields in an area belonged only to members of the same clan. For nomads, who wandered from place to place, it meant that they could follow only a certain prescribed route. The wells along this route were reserved for their clan, and no one else could use them. In the same way, one clan could not take its animals to a well belonging to another clan. In a land with very little water, these rules were meant to avoid conflict between people competing for scarce resources.

When fighting did break out, the clans took charge of restoring the peace. If someone was killed, the clan of the attacker was required to pay a fine to the clan of the victim. A hundred camels was the usual amount for a man, and fifty for a woman. The clan system also played an important role in people's social life. Among the Somaal, marriage within the same clan was frowned upon. It was hoped that if a man and a woman from two different clans married, they would encourage a good relationship between their groups. The Saab, however, usually married within their own clans. As farmers, they remained settled in one area. It was to the clan's advantage to keep the land "all in the family."

The socialist government of Somalia is now trying to break down the clan system. The government believes it damages the nation's unity and makes people less loyal to the central government. So they have taken on many of the clans' traditional roles, one of them being the care of people unable to support themselves. They have also outlawed the paying of fines for murder, and have made that crime punishable by the state. However, old customs are not easily given up. Clans continue to play an important role in Somali life, especially in rural areas.

RELIGION AND CUSTOMS

The vast majority of Somalis are Muslims. It is considered a good deed for a Muslim to make a pilgrimage to the holy city of Mecca. Many Somalis who are too poor to do this make a pilgrimage to the tomb of their clan ancestors instead.

A large number of Somalis continue to hold traditional beliefs. The leader of a clan, for example, is thought to possess a special power called baraka. Baraka is believed to be a gift from God that enables the clan leader to bless his clan. However, baraka is also thought to be dangerous. If a leader from one clan visits another clan, he covers part of his face so that his baraka will not shine too strongly and injure a member of the other clan.

Some Somalis also believe in spirits that cause illness or insanity. According to the legend, an important chief's family, in northeast Somalia, once possessed powerful spirits. When the chief died, his family, fearing they couldn't control the spirits, set them free. To this day, the spirits are believed to roam Somalia and cause trouble. Sneezing, coughing, vomiting, and serious illnesses such as tuberculosis and pneumonia are sometimes blamed on these spirits.

LANGUAGE AND LITERATURE

The Somali people have great respect for language. The ability to say something indirectly rather than openly is much admired. Parents teach their children word games and riddles to encourage this skill, and fathers often ask their would-be sons-in-law trick questions to see how smart they are.

Poetry is practically a national pastime in Somalia. Government leaders are expected to quote lines of poetry in their speeches, or to make up a poem spontaneously to suit an important occasion. Most adults write or know a number of poems, and many of Somalia's modern plays are written as long poems. Poetry is even partly responsible for bringing about Somalia's independence. Poems attacking the colonial powers and calling for the unity of all Somalis helped people believe in their country. Modern works more often speak of love, but politics, women's rights, and sports are also found in Somalia's poetry.

In spite of this great oral tradition, the Somali language had no written form until 1972. Until then anyone who wished to write used their own personal mixture of Arabic and Latin letters. Now, however, there is one standard way of writing Somali, and the government is making great efforts to teach it. In 1974, all Somali schools were closed for several months, and the students went into the countryside to teach everyone the new alphabet. The Somali government estimates that 60 percent of all Somalis can now read and write.

FOOD, CLOTHING, AND HOUSES

Because they are so poor, Somalis are often undernourished. Especially during times of drought, the amount and type of food available is not adequate for good health. The main food of the northern nomads, for example, is camel's milk. During the rainy season, the men who care for the camels away from the main camp may drink 8 or 10 quarts (7 to 9 liters) a day, but eat nothing more than a little grain. The women and children in the main camp live on milk and grain, as well as rice, dates, sugar, and tea. Farmers in southern Somalia eat grains, vegetables, and fruit. Along the coast, fish may be added to the diet. Most Somalis, however, do not get enough meat, fish, or other protein-rich foods.

Somalis who live in cities often wear Western style clothing, but the majority of both men and women wear futas. A futa is a long rectangle of cotton cloth which is wrapped around the lower body like a skirt. Women cover their upper bodies as well, sometimes wearing two or three futas of different colors. As protection from the sun, many Somali men wrap a futa around their heads, turban style. Both men and women wear gold, silver, and carved ivory jewelry. Some wear magical charms—lion's claws, elephant's hair, or shark's teeth wrapped in leather.

A quick walking tour of the capital, Mogadishu, will display the various styles of housing used in all of Somalia. Since many people move to the city looking for work, they build the same type of houses they used in their previous home. Nomads, for example, simply put up collapsible huts. These huts have curved wooden supports that are covered with hides and woven grass mats. When the nomads are ready to move, they can remove the covering and fold up the frame. Farmers, on the other hand, build round huts of mud, ashes, and animal dung. A large center pole supports a cone-shaped, thatched roof.

The newcomers who decide to stay in the city may replace their old houses with large, rectangular buildings made of the same materials as the farmers' huts. These houses are painted white or rose and have metal roofs. As the owners become more prosperous, they replace them with wooden or stone structures.

AGRICULTURE AND INDUSTRY
It would be nice if all Somalis could look forward to a prosperous future. At present, however, they face many serious problems. There is, for example, practically no industry in Somalia. The people are very poor, with an average income of about $150 a

These typical Somali nomad huts are made of
curved wooden frames covered with grass matting.
They are light, cool, and can be easily transported.

year. Three-quarters of the population are herders, raising camels, sheep, goats, and some cattle. In good years they are able to market some meat and animal products for export. However, when weather conditions are bad such as during the drought of the mid-1970s, many nomads starve as their herds die off.

Somalia's farmers are also dependent on the weather. The government is attempting to irrigate more land artificially, but progress is slow. The only export crop is bananas, and much of Somalia's food must be imported. Somalia could someday be self-sufficient, however, if all the farmable land now available were used.

Unfortunately, Somalis traditionally believe that herding is the most dignified occupation. In order to cultivate all the land, some nomads would have to settle in one place and learn to farm. Even if this resulted in a more prosperous life, the nomads would feel they had joined a lower social class. In the same way, not enough has been done to take advantage of the rich fishing grounds off the Somali coast. Until a few years ago, only a few non-Somali groups were fishermen. The Somali government, with aid from other countries, is now sending out modern fishing boats and building a canning factory. However, much more development in this area is needed.

Another hope for the future is oil. Geological surveys show that oil could be hidden under the desert sands of Somalia. Large deposits have yet to be found, but several oil companies are now exploring.

HEALTH AND EDUCATION

A major aim of the present government is to improve health care in Somalia. Because of poor diet and difficult life styles, many Somalis suffer from serious illnesses. It is estimated, for example, that almost 80 percent of young Somali men have tuberculosis. Between one and two hundred thousand people are stricken with malaria each year, and approximately 75 percent of all Somalis have one or more kinds of parasites. Leprosy, tetanus, and polio are also widespread. It is not surprising that even in the late 1970s the average life expectancy for a Somali was only forty-one years. To combat this, the Somali government began operating all health services in 1972. More hospitals are now being built, and many medical workers are being trained. The World Health Organization and other groups are also helping, but much more needs to be done to ensure a healthy future for Somalia.

The earliest Somali schools were religious. Boys and girls attending studied for two years, learning some arithmetic and enough Arabic to read the Koran. After two years, some boys continued to study Arabic and religious law. During the colonial period some Italian and English schools were built, but few Somalis attended. Just before independence, the United Nations helped to establish a system of public schools in Somalia.

After independence, the number of schools grew rapidly. Under the present government, more children—and, in particular, more girls—than ever before are enrolled in school in Somalia. All students receive instruction in reading and writing the Somali language, as well as some sort of vocational training. The number of high schools has also increased. Somali National University provides college level training, although many students go to other countries to study after graduation from high school.

7

DJIBOUTI

On June 27, 1977, Djibouti's new flag was raised for the first time. Each of its four bright colors had a special meaning. Blue was for the sea and sky, and green represented the earth. The white symbolized peace, and the red star symbolized a guide for Djibouti's struggles and hopes.

More than anything else, Djibouti is going to need that star. Although it is the smallest nation in the Horn, in many ways it has the biggest problems. As it begins an era of independence, Djibouti faces a harsh climate, poverty, unemployment, and a location that puts it right in the middle of its neighbors' battles.

THE ISSAS AND AFARS

Djibouti's former name, the French Territory of Afars and Issas, came from the two tribes that live within its borders. Members of both tribes tend to be tall and slim with long oval faces and straight noses. Their skin color ranges from deep black to light brown. The majority of Issas and Afars are nomads, with the Issas traveling mostly in the southern part of Djibouti and the Afars roaming the northern section.

*In 1977, the people of Djibouti cast
their votes for independence from France.*

The Afars tribe itself is much larger than Djibouti's boundaries. In fact, about four-fifths of all Afars live in Eritrea and Ethiopia. As a group, Afars tend to be close-knit and very loyal to their tribe. Nomadic Afars families travel together on a fixed route assigned by the tribe. A family is made up of the husband and wife, the unmarried children, plus the married sons and their wives. Married daughters join their husband's family. Herd and travel routes are passed down from father to son. If there is no male heir, the route is given back to the tribe to be reassigned to another family. Further strengthening the bonds of family is the custom that young men and women marry their first cousins.

The Issas are part of the Somali ethnic group and speak the Somali language. In their travels, nomadic Issas often cross Djibouti's southern border into Somalia. Issas are very hard-working, ambitious people. Although there are fewer of them than the Afars, they hold equal power in Djibouti's government.

Neither tribe, however, has an easy life. Water is extremely scarce, and the green earth of Djibouti's flag is more a wish than a reality. Barren, sandy wastes cover 90 percent of the country. Living in such a difficult climate keeps most nomads on the edge of starvation. Their basic diet is made up of milk and grain. Their herds consist of only those animals that can exist by eating scrub growth of the desert, such as camels, sheep, and goats. Even these animals are eaten only when they become too old to travel with the tribe because they are seen as wealth rather than as food. Unless they are really starving, the nomads would rather keep their herds as large as possible because that gives them a higher social status.

Due to the periodic droughts and ensuing famine, an increasing number of both Afars and Issas have given up their ancient way of life and moved to Djibouti Town, the capital and only major city of the country. Djibouti Town is picturesque, with narrow winding streets and flat-roofed, stone houses. There is an open-air market, and shaded porticoes to walk under. Residents enjoy a more varied diet than nomads, because meat, vegetables, and fruit are imported daily. They can choose from four newspapers, or they can listen to television and radio broadcasts in the official language of French, or in the Afars, Arabic, or Somali tongue.

Yet newcomers to Djibouti Town face enormous challenges. Most nomads have no education or skills suitable for city living. Since Djibouti Town's unemployment rate is over 80 percent, most newcomers find no work at all. The majority of those who do have never handled money before, and are therefore easily cheated. Furthermore, by tribal custom they must share their food with any members of the tribe who are in need. Since everyone in Djibouti has poor relations, any nomad who prospers in the city will soon be supporting a large group.

RELIGION AND EDUCATION

Both Issas and Afars are Muslims. In the city, most people attend at least some religious services. However, among the nomads, the tribe's age-old customs are more carefully followed than newer religious rules. During the Muslim holy month of Ramadan, for example, everyone is supposed to fast from sunrise to sunset. Few of Djibouti's nomads observe the Ramadan fast.

The Muslim religion, however, has had a great effect on Djibouti's educational system. In the past, a few years studying the Koran with a holy man was the only instruction many children ever received. These religious classes were usually held in the open air, near the nomad's tents or in a public street. Children could come and go as they pleased, paying tuition in the form of food and clothing for their teacher.

When Djibouti became a French colony, several Catholic mission schools were opened. About fifty years ago a public school system, staffed mostly by French teachers, was also founded. Both types of schools served few pupils, however, because Djibouti's parents were afraid that the instruction would weaken the faith of their children. Those parents who did allow their sons and daughters to attend often waited until they had had several years of religious instruction first. Consequently, many children began first grade at the age of twelve or thirteen.

The government now allows religious instruction to take place in public school buildings, so that children may study the Koran as well as other subjects. This has helped enrollment, but there is still a long way to go. In the late 1970s, about six thousand students attended primary schools and about two thousand more studied in high school. This represents only a small portion of Djibouti's youth, mainly those who live in the capital. In smaller towns and among the nomads, many children have no opportunity to go to school. This has had serious results: about 90 percent of Djibouti's 250,000 people do not know how to read or write.

INDUSTRY AND TRADE

Aside from two soft drink bottling plants, Djibouti has practically no industry. Moreover, the harsh climate makes farming almost impossible, so nearly all food must be imported. Adding to Djibouti's economic problems are two other imports: refugees and khat.

The Ethiopian-Somali war in the Ogaden has forced more than twenty thousand people to flee to Djibouti in the past few years. These people often arrive with few or no possessions, and they severely strain Djibouti's meager resources. Fortunately, the United Nations commission for refugees and the United States have sent supplies to help.

Khat, a plant that grows in the highlands of Ethiopia, poses a different type of problem. After chewing khat leaves, a person feels "high" and cares less about hunger and the problems of life. Long-term use leads to depression and lowers a person's resistance to disease. Moreover, since khat must be used within two days of picking to have an effect, it has to be flown in daily from Ethiopia. This makes it rather expensive, and an economic problem for Djibouti. The government estimates that up to 40 percent of a person's earnings may be spent on khat, leaving too little for food and other necessities. Although most government leaders recognize the harm that khat is doing to their country, no one really knows how to control it. At present, it is legal and is used by a large portion of the population.

Djibouti's one advantage, however, is its geographical position. Located on the Red Sea, the city of Djibouti makes a convenient port for ships passing through the Suez Canal. In recent years this position has become even more advantageous because the Red Sea is an important shipping lane for oil. Djibouti Town is also a terminal for a railroad that travels to Addis Ababa, Ethiopia's capital city. Ethiopia's only coastline is the war-torn province of Eritrea, so Ethiopia must rely heavily on the Djibouti railroad for trade with the outside world. In a normal year, 40 percent of Ethiopia's exports and 60 percent of its imports pass through Djibouti. The customs duties from these goods provide a major source of income for Djibouti. When anything disrupts the flow of trade, as happened when Eritrean rebels cut off rail service for a time in 1977, Djibouti's economy suffers.

There are several disadvantages to Djibouti's strategic location. It is uncomfortably close to the site of several recent wars. Eritrea lies along Djibouti's northern border, and the Ogaden is to the south. Moreover, foreign powers have often shown great interest in Djibouti's affairs. The world's superpowers are interested in this tiny country because of its nearness to the oil-rich Arabian peninsula. Somalia, which is to the southeast, has claimed part of Djibouti's territory. The Somalis feel that since the Somali-speaking Issas live there, Djibouti should be part of Somalia. With its army hopelessly outnumbered, Djibouti could not hope to resist a Somali invasion.

Djibouti is located on the narrow strait of Bab el Mandeb. Bab el Mandeb is Arabic for "The Gate of Sorrows." As the 1980s begin, Djiboutians can only hope the sorrow will not be theirs.

8
LOOKING TO
THE FUTURE

Djibouti is not the only part of the Horn of Africa that attracts outside attention. Because of their location near the oil-producing lands of the Middle East, the other Horn countries have also concerned the world's superpowers. Sometimes the boiling political situation of the Horn has resulted in confusing changes of alliances. Ethiopia, for example, had been a strong friend of the United States during the reign of Haile Selassie. From 1953 to 1977 America had stationed civilian and military advisers there, and had supplied economic aid for development. However, in February 1977 the United States cut off all military aid to the Mengistu government, charging that there had been many violations of human rights in Ethiopia. Ethiopia quickly expelled the last American government personnel and turned to Moscow for help. In May 1977 Mengistu signed a treaty of "cooperation and friendship" with the Soviet Union. Immediately, Soviet weapons and military advisers poured into Ethiopia to help fight in Eritrea and in the Ogaden. Cuba also sent troops.

Ethiopia's friendship with the Soviet Union and Cuba angered Somalia. As a socialist state, Somalia had had a close alliance with the Soviet Union, and received military aid from that country. They had allowed the Russians to maintain a military base at the Somali port of Berbera. Suddenly in 1977 Somalia found itself defeated in the Ogaden because of the Soviet and Cuban aid to Ethiopia. In retaliation, the Somalis expelled the Soviets from Berbera and began to look to the West for help. The United States agreed to supply arms and other aid, stating that they were to be used for defense of Somalia's frontiers—not for expansion into another country's territory. In August 1980, the United States and Somalia signed a treaty which gave the United States an American base on Somali territory in exchange for foreign aid.

Perhaps because of its bitter history of foreign invasion, Sudan is careful in its relations with outsiders. The Sudanese government has accepted foreign aid from many different nations. In the early years of the Nimieri regime, the Communist party was very powerful, and Sudan and the Soviet Union were strong allies. Recently, however, the Soviet tie is weakening, and Sudan has become closer friends with the United States and western Europe.

The nations of the Horn will have to deal with these foreign influences, as well as with their age-old problems of poverty, hunger, disease, and lack of education. Certainly the people of the Horn of Africa, as they have through their seven thousand year history, will survive.

BOOKS FOR FURTHER READING

Acquaye, Alfred Allotey. *Ethiopia in Pictures*. New York: Sterling Publishing Company, 1973.

Carpenter, Allan and Janis Fortman. *Sudan*. Chicago: Children's Press, 1976.

Edmonds, I. G. *Ethiopia: Land of the Conquering Lion of Judah*. New York: Holt, Rinehart & Winston, 1975.

Ismail, Salah Khogali. *The Sudan In Pictures*. New York: Sterling Publishing Company, 1976.

McKown, Robin. *The Colonial Conquest of Africa*. New York: Franklin Watts, Inc., 1971.

Murphy, E. Jefferson. *Understanding Africa*. Revised edition, New York: Thomas Y. Crowell, 1978.

Vlahos, Olivia. *African Beginnings*. New York: Viking Press, 1967.

INDEX

[63]

Music, in Ethiopia, 30; in Sudan, 37
Muslims, 1, 10, 11, 12, 15–16, 20, 26, 35, 43, 44, 46, 55

Nationalism, Sudanese, 16
Natural resources, in Ethiopia, 31; in Somalia, 50
Nile, 7–9, 10, 34, *see also* Blue Nile; Upper Nile; White Nile
Nimieri, Colonel, 16–17, 60
Nomads, 24, 34, 36–37, 40, 45, 48, 50, 55
Nuba, 35, 37
Nubia, 8, 9
Nuer, 35, 38

Ogaden, 19–20, 23, 30, 57, 58, 59, 60
Omdurman, 36

People's Assembly, in Sudan, 17
Piankhi, 8
Poetry, in Ethiopia, 29–30; in Somalia, 46–47; in Sudan, 37
Prester, John, 11, 12

Ramadan, 55
"Redeemer of the World" church, 10
Refugee problem, 20, 23, 57
Religion, in Djibouti, 55–56, in Ethiopia, 25–26; in Somalia, 46; in Sudan, 35–37

Saab, 44, 45
Sahara Desert, 5
Selassie, Haile, 17, 18, 59
Sennar Dam, 39
Shamas, 29
Shedat, 38

Shilluk, 35
Simen Mountains, 4–5
Sistras, 30
Socialism, in Somalia, 19, 45, 60; in Sudan, 17
Somaal, 44
Somalia, 3, 4, 14, 18–19, 20, 23, 44–51, 54, 55, 58, 60
Soviet Union's influence, 20, 59, 60
Spirits of the Above, 35
Spirits of the Earth, 35
Sudan, 3, 5, 7, 12–13, 14, 15–17, 20, 34–43, 60
Sudd, 5, 13
Suez Canal, 10, 57
Supreme Revolutionary Council, 19

Talmud, 25
Tigre, 24, 25
Tigrinya, 24, 25
Timkat, 25
Topography, 3–5
Tribal territories, 15
Tribe of Dan, 25–26
Tukuls, 29

United Nations, 17, 23, 51, 57
United States' influence, 18, 57, 59, 60
Upper Nile, 13

Wat, 29
Weather, 4, 5
White Nile, 7, 39
World Health Organization, 51

"Yeferas Gooks," 30